Kulin Tales

Seven Seasons of the Bunurong

Sonia Marie

ISBN 978-00646-85537-0
Copyright © Sonia Marie 2022
Copyright © Judy Prosser 2022

All Rights Reserved.
No part of this book may be reproduced or transmitted in any form or by any means, without written permission from the author/artist, including electronic devises.

The rights of the author/artist/publisher have been asserted.

Author © Sonia Marie
Paintings © Judy Prosser, artist
Cover, Design and Layout © Tom Beckers, Sonia Marie and Judy Prosser

Dedication...

This book is dedicated to the four Bunurong women who stood on the foreshore, in the 1820's with their heads held high.

In the dead of night they were stolen; taken by force by boat to a new land.

Even as the roll of the waves took them further away from their home, they remained fierce.

Three began a new life on the islands of the Bass Strait and one went to the islands off the coast of Western Australia.

They all fought for the future of their people and now the future is here, two hundred years later, with the revival of Bunurong language and the written stories of the Kulin People.

I pay my respects to the original four and all of their descendants, past, present and future.

I am honoured to descend from one of the four, with many strong women going before me.

In Memory of Jane, Elizabeth, Marjorie and Eliza.

Sonia Marie 2022

Kulin Tales

Seven Seasons of the Bunurong

Sonia Marie

Introduction - a brief history of the people...

Bunurong people are the Indigenous people of South East Victoria.

Their traditional lands are from Werribee River in the North West, down to Wilsons Promontory in the South East, up to the Dandenong Ranges and back down to the catchments of Old Carrum Swamp, Tarwin River and Westernport Bay. Bunurong land also takes in Mornington Peninsula and French and Phillip Island.

Bunurong people are part of a language group or nation known as Kulin/Koolin.
This nation has 5 language groups of which Bunurong is one.

The first British settlement on Bunurong country occurred at Sullivan Bay 1803 and by 1839 the Bunurong had, sadly, been reduced to approx 80-90 people living on their Traditional Country.

By 1863, a small handful of Bunurong, joined other surviving leaders of the Kulin Nation and squatted on a traditional camping site near Healesville ,which became known as Coranderrk Station and here they stayed.

Sadly after a while, Bunurong people were no longer recorded in numbers.

The only recorded, surviving Bunurong from this date, are the descendants of the woman stolen by the sealers, in the early 1800's and taken to the Bass Strait.

Yain Yang

Dance & Song

Weeyukabul N'Yo'Weenth - Old Man Sun... Jan/Feb

It is the season of **Weeyukabul N'Yo'Weenth**, (Old Man Sun), where the movements of the people are led by the stars in the Northern sky.

Now is the time for the Kulin people to prepare for **Yain Yang**, (dance and song). It is ceremony time.

Take your eyes to the **Boorurn** (sky)map. **Moonmoondiik**, (Pleides Constellation) is visible now and you can see Orion nearby, wearing his belt and tools. This signals the **Baggarooks**, (women), young girls and the **Cooleenth**, (men) and **Yanyean**, (boys) to separate. Coming of age ceremonies begin and the people won't see each other again until the end of season's dance.

Communication is done between the groups with small **Weenths**, (fires), seen flickering at night up and down the coastline. Each one lets their family group know, everyone is safe. It is a sacred time and the people have been preparing for many weeks.

Hot **Moornmoot**, (winds), blow across the **Beek**, (country) now, the **N'Yo'weenth**, (sun) is high. The **Bargan**, (cool) night air, travels across **Warrain**, (The Ocean) and brings relief from the daytime heat.

Bulgana, (meat), is smoked and hung out to dry in preparation for the colder months. Camps are near large, fresh waterholes and **Touit** (fish), Snapper, Flounder, **Eoke** (eels), and Abolone are in abundance at this time of year. All that seafood needs to be mixed with plant food to keep the tummy healthy and settled, so tubers are collected from the Murnong, Lillies and Warrigul Greens, Sea Celery and **Karkalla**, (pig face) are added to the evening meal with fruit from the **Morr** (prickly, Currant Bush).

Eepaeep (native raspberry), and **Ballart** (Cherry Ballart), are picked by the **Boopoops** (children), their **Beenaks** (baskets), filled with sweet berries. Gum from the Wattle and Eucalyptus, is collected and stored in the hollows of trees along walking tracks, to be used in the future for burns, tummy aches and, where necessary, making repairs to tools and spears.

A special drink called **Beal** (ceremonial drink), is made, to get ready for the coming-together dance. Holes are dug and sealed, then flowers from the **Dargurn** (Yellow Box), and River Red Gum are added to soak and ferment.

As the Kulin people lie under the bright night **Boorurn** (sky), their fires burning, stories are told and lessons learnt. Venus and **Meniyan** (moon), is close now and meteor showers can be seen streaking their bright lights across the country. Many shooting **Tutbyrums** (stars), fall at this time of year; many wishes are made and many whispers to the ancestors can be heard through the quiet of night.

All is well in Bunurong Country.

Monomeeth - Good Autumn... March/April

Welcome to the season of **Monomeeth** (good autumn), where day and night are equal. Where you can hear the call of the **Nayook** (Black Cockatoo), as he collects the water from **Warrain** (the ocean), weaving his magic, he brings the rain to the Balluk (people). **Bellin** (Currawong), begins his call, bringing the cold down the mountain. Together with **Nayook** and the **Balluk** (the people), they will start the **Ba'anth Mellaba** (rain), that will fall over Bunurong country throughout **Monomeeth** (autumn).

Bunurong people begin to set up camps for warmth and weather protection, coming together in larger groups, as now is the time to prepare skins for rugs and cloaks. Skins from **Walert** (brush tailed possum), and **Koim** (Kangaroo), are woven together as people sit and share stories around **Weenth** (fire).

Soon it will be **Moonbird** (mutton bird), season and celebrations take place for the **Eoke** (Eel), season as harvest has been plentiful.

Monomeeth is the time when the **Wurun** (Manna gum), flower and **Booboops** (children), get their fingers sticky with **Murrub** (lerps), and honey.

The landscape begins to glow from soft, cool burns as it is now a safe time to tidy the floor of the **Beek** (earth), night dew has returned and the **Weenth**, will encourage the rain to come.

Koim (kangaroo), are caught for skin and meat to be stored before **Dumbalk** (winter).

Bambra (mushrooms), begin to appear and eyes are turned downward for food on the forest floor.

Bullin Bullin (lyrebird), begin their courtship dance and feathers are traded amongst the Kulin people for ceremony.

Wake early now, before the sun rises; look to the **Boorurn** (sky), to see the twinkling path of the Milky Way and the teeny tiny **Tutbyrum** (stars).

This is the time when we are allowed a glimpse into the the centre of the galaxy.

Warrain

Ocean

Wyeeboo Dumbalk - Early Winter... May

We are in the time of **Wyeeboo Dumbalk** (early winter). The Yallock-Bulluk people have begun their journey to Cape Woolamia on **Korri'Yong** (Phillip Island). It is here the **Weeyukabul** (old people), will sit and **Yain Yang** (sing), a special song, a song of giants that glisten and cast shadows across the surface of the cold blue **Warrain** (Ocean). A welcome song, for it is a time for **Beta'Yil** (whale), to arrive... she has travelled far, following the contours of the **Warrain** (ocean) floor, to find her way here now, to rest and raise her calves in the warmer water. As she dances so do the people.

Cooleenth (men), can be seen now, using their bark canoes, travelling between the islands for **Dirundirri** (eggs), **Korrman** (seal) meat, and **Touit** (fish).

The **Baggarooks** (women), are also busy for they are master divers and are seen swimming between the sea caves and reefs that are hidden under the high tide for it is here that they fill their **Pellongs** (nets), with mussels and oysters to be cooked later on the open fire.

Wyeeboo Dumbalk, where freezing **Moornmoot** (winds), begin to creep in from the south, where flying **Boorans** (ants), are seen, carried lightly on the wind and **Bamu** (Ring Tailed Possum), can be found with her tiny babies in the drey.

Animal fat is collected and stored now. It will be used later to rub into the skin to keep the people warm when the colder months come.

A short trip to **Moonarmia** (Churchill Island), is planned. It is the place that holds the story of the Moonah Tree and forbidden love. It is here that **Woorap** (ochre), is gathered for dance and ceremony.

Glance around the animal world now. In the distance **Yirrangin** (Dingo), can be heard for breeding season is here and young males are calling for love. Tiny **Warrans** (sugar gliders), are born now and in amongst the mangoes and mudflats of **Warn'Maring** (Western Port Bay).

Wadjil (Pelican), **Bayba'djerruk** (Ibis), Heron and Spoonbill, add colour and song to the wildlife that make their home amongst the waters of the bay.

Winjeel (White Bellied Sea Eagle), ancestor to all birds; see him soar across the grey misty sky as he floats along the edge of **Warn'maring**, hunting, for now is breeding season and his wife waits for him.

The smell of the salt in the air mixed with the crisp, cool breeze makes this a **Monomeeth** (good time), to be on **Korri'Yong** (Phillip Island), one of the most beautiful places on the earth.

The Kulin people are busy now, preparing for **Dumbalk**, cloaks are repaired, **Weenth** (fires), are lit, food is stored for the **Dumbalk** (cold/winter).

There is much to be grateful for.

Bullarto Dumbalk - Plenty Cold/Winter... June/July

Bullarto Dumbalk (plenty winter), is here. Days are short, nights are long. **Wyeeboo Lark** (low, thin, mist), falls over the tops of the tall trees; the temperature is low.

Bellin (Currawong), tells his story. He is the guardian of the **Cabbin** (cold). You will hear him bring the frost on his breathe and in his call. Bunurong people have settled into warm sheltered **Mya'mya**s (houses), **Willums**, (camps), are either, inside rock caves or in clearings amongst the woodlands.

The **Beek** (country), near the rivers and creeks, is often flooded the lowlands wet and cold.

Moornmoot (wind), blows in strong from the south, because of this, **Willums** (camps), are built amongst the shelter of **Koran'warnambul** (the Dandenong Ranges)

Food is no longer gathered from the **Warrain** (ocean), rather, hunted from the land. **Koim** (Kangaroo), is fat, so now is a good time to hunt; nothing is wasted. Small animals are snared, yams are harvested along with bush onions and **Bambra** (mushrooms). Winter orchids are everywhere.

A lot of time is spent around the **Weenth** (fire). **Weeyukabul** (Elders/old people), use this time to teach. There are important lessons in **Beenak** (basket), weaving, artefact and tool manufacture. Cloaks from **Koim** (kangaroo), are stitched together and used for warmth.

In the animal kingdom, we see **Birrith Birrith** (masked plover), begin to build their nests, **Warren** (wombat), is emerging and can be seen fattening up on the tussock grass as well as dry leaves and **Bambra** (mushrooms). **Bath'mun** (wood duck), are seen on the lakes and Powerful Owl, nests in the large hollows amongst the forest trees. **Waaki** (crow), often solitary, can be seen flying in pairs at this time. Many animals are pairing up, preparing for **Dumbalk** (winter), and breeding season.

Look to the **Tutbyrum** (stars), as we come into the constellation of **Bunjil**, (Eagle).

It is the time to sit still, take in the **Dumbalk** sounds, look up to the **Boorurn** (sky), to see **Meniyan** (moon), so close now.

It is the season of family.

Bam'mil

Emu

Wyeeboo Pareip - Early Spring... August

Muryan (Silver Wattle), has begun to flower; the cold weather will soon end.

We watch *N'Yo'weenth* (sun), as she gathers her *Woorap* (Ochre), to paint the sky in shades of red and orange. She knows it is the time of rain and *Moornmoot* (wind), but she stops to kiss the tops of the *Wurran* (Mountain Ash), and bring her warmth to the *Beek* (earth), unfreezing *Dumbalk* (winter).

She uses her warmth to calls in the spread of the *Guling* (orchid), to let us know it is now the season of *Wyeeboo Pareip* (early spring).

The Bunurong people will follow the *Boorurn* (sky), map and wait for the *Bam'mil* (emu), to stand up from the nest in the night sky; it is then the babies will be ready and we will see the *Garrong* (Black Wattle), drop its flowers into the rivers and streams that flow down from *Koran'warnambul* (Dandenong Ranges), into the bay.

This is the season of the nesting birds. *Dirundjirri* (bird's eggs), are collected as they are an important food source now. *Garrong* (Black Wattle), is connected to *Koon'warra* (Swan), for they share the same story. Black Wattle lets us know the swan eggs are ready and our plans to journey down the hill towards *Warn'maring* (Western Port), and the *Warrain* (Ocean), will soon begin.

In the animal kingdom *Queeop Queeop* (birds), are busy building and guarding nests. *Karbora* (Koala), will soon start his night song, looking for *Quinkee Monomeeth* (love and affection), and the Echidna trains will begin, with many males following the one woman across the land.

Food for the people is in abundance right now, with the *Baggarook* (woman), and *Booboops* (children), collecting *Mel'lurk* (grubs), *Bambra* (mushrooms), small marsupials and the *Komba'derk* (soft tree fern), all of this mixed with meat and cooked over *Weenth* (fire), under the *Tutbyrums* (stars), brings a good life for the people.

Everyone sits together as a family now and makes their plans for *Pareip* (spring), when they will head towards the ocean and once again come together in large groups to *Yain Yang* (Dance/Ceremony), and care for country.

Look to the stars right now *Bunjil* (eagle), is still close and *Meniyan* (moon), even closer. Sit *Nurring'ian* (quietly/do not speak).

You are here in this moment of time and all is good.

Pareip - Spring... September - October

Pareip (spring), is here and flowers are opening everywhere. Keep your eyes out for the **Barroworn**, (magpie), they are protecting their young now, as it is the season of the nesting birds.

Garrong (Black Wattle), slowly begin to flower, dropping their flowers in the running water, let the Bunurong who are now down in the low lands, know that the **Koon-warra** (swan), eggs are ready to collect.

It is the return time of the **Eoke** (eel), which brings much celebration and **Yain Yang** (dance). The **Baggarook** (women), decorate their hair with the flowers of the **Murnong** (yams) and the Kangaroo Apple. **Murnong**, the wild yams are beginning to flower, indicating the tubers are nearly ready to eat.

Murnalong (bees), are swarming and the **Beek** (country), is filled with the sound of movement as the birds and animals awake with the return of the **N'Yo'weenth** (sun).

As the days warm, beautiful **Bollam Bollam** (butterfly), emerge and the Bunurong begin to set up **Willum** (camp), closer to the **War-rain** (ocean), where they can enjoy fishing from the rocks and eat an abundance of green, leafy foods, readily available.

It is now the time where day and night are equal and colour returns to the land.

Pareip; my favourite time of year.

Bullarto N'Yo'Weenth - Plenty Sun... Nov/Dec

We are now entering into the season known as **Bullarto N'Yo'Weenth** (plenty sun) - (early summer).

Bunurong people begin to welcome their neighbours to the coast, people swim and gather **Tuyang** (shellfish), and **Pidderon** (periwinkles), from the rocky platforms or fish for snapper at the mouth of the mangrove inlets, mixing the days catch with the fruit of the **Karkala** (pigface), and sweet tubers that the **Baggarook** (women), gather.

Cooleenth (men), will sit together, making bark canoes so they could travel to the islands to catch **Koorman** (seal). **Moonbird** (muttonbird), have arrived and soon, will lay their single egg.

The Kulin people gather together their camps, getting ready for the coming of age ceremonies. Many **Yain Yangs** (corroboree), and **Weenth** (fires), burn brightly across the landscape.

It is an abundant time for the Kulin people, native grasses grow tall and seed now and **Murrab** (lerps), can be collected from **Wurran** (Manna Tree). Bulbs are ready for harvesting and the **Bollam Bollam**, (butterflies), add colour to the fields of wildflowers.

Doonburrim (lizards and snakes), are active and **Eoke** (eels), begin to swim down the river. People stay near the fresh water sources as the **N'Yo'Weenth** (sun), begins to heat up.

Kulin **Beek**,(country), is bursting with life.

Glossary of Words - Kulin Tales

Ba'anth Mellaba - Rain
Barroworn - Magpie
Bam`mil - Emu
Bambra - Mushroom
Bamu - Ring Tailed Possum
Bath`mun - Wood Duck
Balluk - People
Ballart - Cherry Ballart
Bargan - cool
Baggarooks - Women
Bayba`djerruk - Ibis
Beal - Special Ceremony drink
Beek - Country
Beenaks - Baskets
Bellin - Currawong
Beta`yil - Whale
Birrith Birrith - Masked Plover
Boorurn - sky
Booran - Ant
Bollam Bollam - Butterfly
Booboops - Babies/small children
Bulgana - Meat
Bullin Bullin - Lyrebird
Bullarto - Plenty
Bunyil - Eagle
Cabbin - Cold
Cooleenth - Men

Dargun - Yellow Box Tree
Dirun`djirri - bird eggs
Doonburrim - Lizard
Dumbalk - Cold/Winter
Eepaeep - Native Raspberry
Eoke - Eel
Garrong - Black Wattle
Guling - Orchid
Karbora - Koala
Karkalla - Pigface
Koim - Kangaroo
Komba`derk - Soft tree fern
Korrman - Seal
Korri`Yong - Phillip Island
Koran`Warnambul - The Dandenong Ranges
Koon`warra - Swan
Mel`lurk - Grubs
Meniyan - Moon
Moonarmia - Churchhill Island
Moorn`moot - Wind
Moonmoondiik - Pleides Constellation
Monomeith - Good
Morr - Prickly Currant Bush
Murnalong - Bee
Murnong - Yam
Muryan - Silver Wattle
Murrub - Lerps

Mya`Mya - House
Nayook - Cockatoo
Nurring`ian - Quiet/do not speak
N`yo`Weenth - Sun
Pareip - Spring
Pellongs - Nets
Pidderon - Periwinkles
Queeop Queeop - Birds
Quinkee Monomeith - love/affection
Touit - Fish
Tutbyrums - Stars
Tuyang - Shellfish
Waaki - Crow
Wad`jil - Pelican
Warren - Wombat
Warn`maring - Western Port Bay
Walert - Brush Tail Possum
Warrain - Ocean
Warrans - Sugar Gliders
Weenth - Fire
Weeyukabul - Old Man
Winjeel - White Bellied Sea Eagle
Willum - Camp
Wyeeboo - Early
Wyeeboo Lark - Low, thin mist
Woorap - Ochre
Wurun - Manna Gum

Wurrum - Mountain Ash
Yan Yean - Boys
Yain Yang - Dance and Song
Yirrangin - Dingo

Monomeeth Mirambeena...

(which in language means thank you or good you.)

Monomeeth Mirambeena... without these people and their support, I could not have done this...

Mya're, Tal'ly'a, Tjitjin and Kara... my four, beautiful children.
Aunty Verna Nichols
Uncle Mervyn Brown
Judy Prosser
Tom Beckers
Stephen Compton, Kat and Kye
Charlie and Haylie Blomley
My sister Phaedra
Toni Benetti
Bette, Frank and Galen.
Bridget Weaver.
Stacey Demarco

My Elders, Past and Present and family in Tasmania and Victoria... this one's for you!

About the Author...

Sonia Marie, was born on King Island. Her mother, a Bunurong woman, her father a Scottish man.

Over the past twenty-five years, she has dedicated her time and passion to the revival of her community's language and its written history.

She began to weave Traditional Language throughout her work to keep her culture alive and to help hold doors open for her people in the future.

With her work as a herbalist... and her love of plants and history, Sonia also teaches classes to the general public, through her business, Dance of the Plants.

She currently lives and works on Kulin Country... with her three children, her garden and her dogs.

The Paintings

Cover painting - **"Spirit Girl"** - Acrylic on Canvas - 90 cm x 90 cm

Weeyukabul N'Yo'Weenth - **"Desert Moon Dance"** - Acrylic on Canvas - 61 cm x 61 cm

Monomeeth - **"Corroboree in the firelight"** - Acrylic on Canvas - 51 cm x 61 cm

Wyeeboo Dumbalk - **"Whaleshark Girl"** - Watercolour and Gouache on Arches - 20 cm x 38 cm

Bullarto Dumbalk - **"Nightwatch"** - Watercolour and Gouache on Arches - 38 cm x 58 cm

Wyeeboo Pareip - **"Emu Dancer"** - Watercolour and Gouache on Arches - 42.5 cm x 38 cm

Pareip - **"River Idyll"** - Acrylic on Belgian Linen - 61 cm x 76 cm

Bullarto N'Yo'Weenth - **"Lake Fishing Spot"** - Acrylic on Canvas - 51 cm x 76 cm

About the Artist...

Judy Prosser, has lived in the Kimberley for over 40 years, but has travelled extensively all over Australia, with her sketchbook at hand.

She lives and paints, mostly in the outback regions around Broome and the Kimberley, WA; Darwin and the Northern Territory; Cairns and Far North Queensland.

Her sketches become paintings in her studio, on her remote station home, next to the mighty Fitzroy River.

She especially likes to show how humans can be in harmony with nature, and in her work, likes to portray a connection, an interaction, and a happy relationship between humans and the native creatures of the Australian wilderness.

Judy also has a passion for horses, and her little dog Mallee, who is always at her side.

www.ingramcontent.com/pod-product-compliance
Lightning Source LLC
Chambersburg PA
CBHW050854010526
44107CB00048BA/1608